MODERN ERAS
the early
1960s
to the mid
1970s
· UNCOVERED ·

From Beatlemania to Watergate

Sean Sheehan

Raintree

www.raintreepublishers.co.uk
Visit our website to find out more information about **Raintree** books.

To order:
☎ Phone 44 (0) 1865 888113
🖹 Send a fax to 44 (0) 1865 314091
🖥 Visit the Raintree Bookshop at **www.raintreepublishers.co.uk** to browse our catalogue and order online.

First published in Great Britain by Raintree, Halley Court, Jordan Hill, Oxford, OX2 8EJ, part of Harcourt Education.
Raintree is a registered trademark of Harcourt Education Ltd.

Editorial: Melanie Copland and Lucy Beevor
Design: Michelle Lisseter and Bridge Creative Services Ltd
Picture Research: Mica Brancic and Ginny Stroud-Lewis
Production: Duncan Gilbert

Originated by Chroma Graphics (Overseas) Pte. Ltd
Printed and bound in China by South China Printing Company

ISBN 1 844 43955 0 (hardback)
10 09 08 07 06
10 9 8 7 6 5 4 3 2 1

British Library Cataloguing in Publication Data
Sheehan, Sean
From Beatlemania to Watergate. – (Modern Eras Uncovered)
909.8'26

A full catalogue record for this book is available from the British Library.

Acknowledgements
Associated Press p. **43**; Bettmann/Corbis p. **8**; Corbis/Bettmann pp. **6, 7, 14, 18, 23, 27, 32, 33, 37, 38, 48**; Corbis/Henry Diltz p. **4**; Corbis/Hulton Deutsch Collection pp.**16–17**; Corbis/Lynn Goldsmith pp. **44, 49**; Corbis/Wally McNamee pp.**28, 47**; Getty Images pp.**12, 39, 40**; Getty Images/Hulton Archive pp. **9, 22, 25, 26, 34, 41**; Getty Images/Time Life Pictures pp. **21, 29**; Redferns Music Picture Library p.**5**; Rex Features pp.**13, 36, 42**; The Art Archive/Dagli Orti © Tom Wesselmann/VAGA, New York/DACS, London 2004 p.**10**; The Bridgeman Art Library (Private Collection) © The Andy Warhol Foundation for the Visual Arts, Inc/DACS, London, 2004. Trademarks Licensed by Campbell Soup Company. All Rights Reserved, p.**11**; The Kobal Collection/MGM p.**35**; The Kobal Collection/Warner Brothers p.**46**; Topfoto pp.**30, 31**.

Cover photograph (top) reproduced with permission of Corbis/Hulton-Deutsch Collection, and photograph (bottom) reproduced with permission of Corbis/Wally McNamee.

CONTENTS

Any words appearing in the text in bold, **like this**, are explained in the glossary.

GOOD TIMES, BAD TIMES

The Beatles pop group were very popular in the early 1960s and their fame spread around the world. They became instantly recognizable as an image of the "swinging sixties." It was a time when there was much to celebrate and enjoy, especially for young people. The teenagers of the early 1960s had no memories of the Second World War (1939–1945), being born in the years of peace that followed the fighting. They were enjoying the prosperity that came to many parts of the world after the end of the war. This prosperity was first experienced in the United States, and by the early 1960s it had reached Europe and beyond.

For the first time, young people had their own money to spend and they were able to dress differently and listen to new kinds of music. Along with these new fashions were new forms of architecture and art. More importantly, young people were no longer following the traditions of their parents. In the late 1960s, people started to rebel against traditional society. This was the age of **hippies** and **flower power**, and the birth control pill. The popular American musician Bob Dylan summed up the era in an album called *The times they are a-changin'* which was released in 1964.

The times, however, were not always changing for the best. The sixties was also a period of violence. Headlines shocked the world with news of politicians being **assassinated** in public. This was also the period when people realized the nature of the threat posed by **nuclear weapons**. The year 1968 saw large demonstrations by young people who wanted to change the world and stop a war that was raging in Vietnam.

Dozens of hippies dance in a field at Renaissance Fair during the 1960s. Many wear flowers in their hair, which symbolised their desire to get back to the beauty of nature.

As 1969 came to an end, it seemed to spell the end of a whole era of **optimism**. The early years of the next decade brought a more sober and depressing period. The **Cold War** rivalry between the United States and the **USSR** started to make itself felt once more, and conflict in Northern Ireland erupted into brutal violence. The mood of joyful celebration associated with Beatlemania ended in 1974 with the Watergate affair and the resignation of a US president. Politics seemed like a dirty business and people were **disenchanted**.

"The times they are a-changin' "

"Come mothers and fathers throughout the land
And don't criticise what you can't understand.
Your sons and your daughters are beyond your command,
Your old world is rapidly agein'.
Please get out of the new one if you can't lend your hand,
For the times they are a-changin'. "

(FROM BOB DYLAN'S SONG "THE TIMES THEY ARE A-CHANGIN' ")

Bob Dylan became a spokesman for a generation in the 1960s, and millions of young people embraced his lyrics in the song, "The times they are a-changin'."

THE SWINGING SIXTIES

By the start of the 1960s, the UK's **economy** was healthy and looked set to stay that way. Throughout the 1950s wages had been gradually rising. Unemployment was low, working people were living better than their parents, and young people were taking the good times for granted. People were enjoying more than a one-week annual holiday and owning a second-hand car was a reachable ambition for working families. Factories were churning out new appliances – washing machines, refrigerators, televisions, vacuum cleaners – in greater numbers than ever before.

The Beatles chat with television host Ed Sullivan between rehearsals for their first live US TV performance, 9 February 1964.

Beatlemania

"Please Please Me" was the second single released by The Beatles, a young band from Liverpool, and it went to the top of the UK charts in 1963. What was to become known as Beatlemania started in February of the following year when the band arrived in New York. The story goes that when the band members first saw thousands of young people waiting at the airport they thought someone important must have been on their plane. They did not realize the fans were there to welcome them.

Two days later, when The Beatles performed on *The Ed Sullivan Show*, they were watched by a US audience of over 70 million. When they made their first live performance in the United States a few days later, their fans screamed and cried with delight just like their audiences back in the UK. In time, the screaming of fans made it difficult for The Beatles to even hear themselves perform and it added to their decision to stop touring. Their last performance was in San Francisco in 1966, although they went on releasing hugely popular studio albums until they split up in 1970.

The Beatles – John Lennon, Paul McCartney, George Harrison, and Ringo Starr – atttracted criticism as well as huge numbers of fans. In 1966, when John Lennon said they were more popular than Jesus, they outraged some religious groups in the United States. Despite any criticism, their popularity has lasted and no other band has had so much influence on **popular culture**.

The Beatles' fans scream at the top of their lungs during the famous concert at Shea Stadium, New York, United States, 16 August 1965.

The Beatles' albums

Please Please Me (1963)
With the Beatles (1963)
A Hard Day's Night (1964)
Beatles for Sale (1964)
Help! (1965)
Rubber Soul (1965)
Revolver (1966)
Sgt. Pepper's Lonely Hearts Club Band (1967)
Magical Mystery Tour (1967) (Double EP)
The Beatles (White Album) (1968)
Yellow Submarine (1969)
Abbey Road (1969)
Let It Be (1970)

Transatlantic music

There were many other bands and singers who achieved success during the early 1960s. In the UK, The Rolling Stones were the next most popular band and they, too, made a big impact in the United States. The music of United States' groups such as The Supremes and The Temptations, and singers such as Aretha Franklin and Marvin Gaye, became very popular in the UK.

Fab fashions

In the early 1960s, for the first time in history, fashion was greatly influenced by young people. New designers sensed that young people wanted to break with the past, and dress in exciting and original ways. What was happening, people said, was "fab" – short for fabulous.

Miniskirts and button-downs

The miniskirt became a worldwide success even though older people thought it was **immoral** and unfeminine. Clothes became startlingly colourful, for men as well as women, with striped T-shirts and wide floral ties becoming popular. Frilled shirts, button-down collars, and longer hair became fashionable for men. Carnaby Street in London, UK, became famous for its clothes shops and young people flocked there to see the latest fashions, which also became popular in shops in US cities.

Singer Nancy Sinatra performs for US troops in South Vietnam, in the mid 1960s, wearing a fab minidress and knee-length boots.

Pop star fashions

Pop music had a tremendous impact on fashion. The Beatles' style of dress, as well as their hairstyles, were copied by trendy teenagers. Other musicians, such as the Rolling Stones and Jimi Hendrix, developed more **flamboyant** styles of dress and these also became very popular. Female pop stars, such as Nancy Sinatra, followed the fashion for the rising hemlines of miniskirts, patterned stockings and high boots, black eye make-up, and white lipstick.

New materials

Disposable paper dresses and **vinyl** clothing that flashed in time to pop music were invented, but they were not very popular! Advances in technology made it easy to produce **synthetic** materials such as acrylic. This material allowed clothes to dry crinkle-free, with very little need for ironing. Plastic was another cheap material that was easily produced, and it was used to make furniture, television casings, phone booths, and raincoats.

Looking to the sky

The sense of glamour that affected clothes designers also influenced the designers of buildings. Adventurous architects wanted to show off with new ways of using glass, steel and concrete. Some of the finest buildings were designed at this time, such as the World Trade Center in New York, United States. The designs were simple, with clean lines and an uncluttered style. Others, such as the Post Office Tower in London, aimed to be futuristic by displaying electronic gadgets.

The modern and futuristic-looking Post Office Tower in London was finished in 1964. It is now known as the BT Tower.

Mods and Rockers

In the 1960s, two rival teenage groups emerged with completely opposite tastes in fashion and music. The Mods were attracted to the elegant clothing of modern jazz musicians, and copied their style. Mod boys dressed in simple suits, drainpipe trousers, and suede shoes. Mod girls wore dark eye make-up, and cut their hair short. Bands such as the Who and the Small Faces became associated with the Mod movement as it grew more popular.

Rockers, on the other hand, listened to American rock and roll singers, such as Elvis Presley and Buddy Holly. They had a "bad boy" image, and their fashion included jeans, studded leather jackets, and pointy shoes called winkle pickers.

There were several battles between the Mods and Rockers, most notably in Brighton, UK, in 1964. The Rockers were defeated and were never again at the forefront of fashion. Mods, however, went on to influence the fashions of **Ska** bands in the 1980s.

Pop art

The music of groups such as The Beatles was pop music. "Pop" was short for "popular" – because so many people enjoyed listening to this music. Soon, the way ordinary people lived and enjoyed themselves became known as popular culture. So, when artists in the 1960s began using objects of everyday life in their paintings, their work became known as pop art. Pop art seemed to celebrate the new age of **mass produced** goods, colour photography, and advertising images.

The art of the swinging sixties

Pop art can be recognized by the bright, flat colours and the sharp lines used to represent famous people and everyday objects such as hamburgers and television sets. Strong colours were more important to the artists than strong feelings about what they were painting. Instead of expressing an emotion, pop artists seemed happy to play with images of mass-produced consumer goods and pop or film stars.

Aspects of the new art were first noticeable in the late 1950s, in both the United States and the UK. One of the early pop artists was Peter Blake. He was asked to produce the album cover for a new and important collection of songs by The Beatles called *Sergeant Pepper's Lonely Hearts Club Band*. This became one of the most recognizable album covers ever.

Still life no 59, by the pop artist Tom Wesselmann, is a typical example of the bright colours and everyday objects used in this type of art.

Andy Warhol

In the United States, one of the most important pop artists was Andy Warhol. He became famous for combining painting with photography to produce multiple images of one-dollar bank notes, cans of soup, and figures of stars such as Marilyn Monroe and Elvis Presley. Other pop artists created sculptures, using cloth and other materials, as well as the traditional clay. It was a time to experiment with art.

> "Everything is beautiful. Pop is everything."
>
> "In the future everyone will be world-famous for fifteen minutes."
>
> "When I got my first television set, I stopped caring so much about having close relationships."
>
> (ANDY WARHOL)

This is Andy Warhol's famous artwork called *Campbell's Soup Cans*, from 1965.

Colourful art

Pop art was new, cool art for a new world. Places such as Eastern Europe and China, however, which did not share in the prosperity of the West, did not develop a similar art form. Pop art became an expression of the culture and the way of life of the West.

People wanted colour in their lives, and new designs for everyday living began to spread from the United States to western Europe, especially the UK. The idea of an "open plan" home, with large rooms and windows instead of many small rooms, became popular. New materials, often using new forms of plastic, began to be used for home decoration and furniture. Pop art, which had little in common with traditional ideas about art, was a part of this new way of living and looking at life.

A feeling of change and improvement was affecting UK politics. In 1960, the Labour Party voted in favour of abolishing nuclear weapons, although the party leader reversed this decision the following year. Labour narrowly won the 1964 general election under Harold Wilson. By this time, the UK's leaders and politicians were coming to terms with the fact that the UK was no longer a **superpower**.

The Cold War

Rivalry and distrust between the United States and the USSR resulted in them taking up opposite sides in various conflicts that developed around the world in the decades after the end of the Second World War in 1945. Permanently hostile towards one another, the two superpowers never actually fought face to face and so their conflict was called the Cold War. In 1962, this came extremely close to a "hot war," one that would be fought with the deadly nuclear weapons that both superpowers were developing in an **arms race**.

Cuban missile crisis

Until Cubans, under their leader Castro, seized power in 1959, a **corrupt** US-backed dictator called Batista ruled Cuba. The United States was outraged when US-owned factories and properties in Cuba were **nationalized**. It cut off trade with Cuba and helped supporters of Batista in a failed attempted invasion of the island (known as the Bay of Pigs after the beach they landed on) in 1961. Cuba turned to the USSR for aid and protection and in this way, Cuba became involved in the Cold War.

The United States had nuclear weapons based in Turkey. Fired from here, they could reach the USSR, so the **Soviet** leader, Khrushchev, got permission from Castro to ship Soviet nuclear missiles to Cuba. This alarmed the United States because from Cuba the missiles could easily reach US cities.

A US patrol plane flies over a Soviet ship during the Cuban missile crisis, 27 October 1962.

President John F. Kennedy meets with the Soviet leader, Khrushchev, after the drama of the Cuban missile crisis had died down.

A crisis developed when President Kennedy of the United States demanded the missiles be removed. The days that followed, 20–27 October 1962, were extremely tense, with the world on the verge of a nuclear war. The United States assembled the largest invasion force since the Second World War. US planes carrying nuclear weapons were kept in the air, ready to target the USSR the moment the order came. Soviet forces on Cuba were put on full alert. As the fear of war and the use of nuclear weapons spread, a wave of panic buying swept across the United States, as people stocked up with supplies of food and water.

Khrushchev eventually backed down and agreed to remove the missiles from Cuba. Kennedy agreed to remove missiles from Turkey – though he did not allow this fact to be made public at the time. Kennedy also agreed not to try and invade Cuba again. This agreement made Kennedy look like the stronger leader who had forced Khrushchev to back down.

The death of a president

John F. Kennedy was only 43 when he became the youngest US president in 1961. He and his wife, Jacqueline, seemed to represent the glamour and optimism of the time. JFK, as he was popularly known, was handsome and dynamic but, barely a thousand days into his presidency, he was shot dead in Dallas, Texas. It was 22 November 1963.

President John F. Kennedy and his wife, Jacqueline, ride in an open-topped car through Dallas, Texas, United States, 22 November 1963. Moments later, the President was assassinated.

11:37 a.m.: Air Force One, the airplane carrying Kennedy, touches down at Love Field Airport outside Dallas. Soon after, the President takes his seat in an open-topped limousine with his wife next to him.

12:29: The limousine makes its way along Houston Street and turns left into Elm Street, passing the Texas Schoolbook Depository. Suddenly, half a minute past the half hour, a sharp crack is heard and a bullet enters Kennedy's neck. A second shot hits a man in the front seat of the car. A third shot hits Kennedy in the head and he is killed.

12:32: A police patrolman, alerted by a police message, makes his way up the stairs of the Depository building with the building supervisor. They spot a man on the second floor who is later identified as Lee Harvey Oswald. On the sixth floor, a rifle is found near a window overlooking Elm Street.

1:15 p.m.: A police officer is shot dead after challenging a man acting suspiciously.

1:40: Oswald is seen entering a cinema six blocks from the place where the policeman was shot. A suspicious bystander calls the police and Oswald is arrested ten minutes later.

On 24 November 1963, Oswald was shot dead by Jack Ruby, during a jail move. Ruby was a local nightclub owner and Kennedy supporter. It was the first televised murder because news cameras had already been covering the story.

A shocked world

Political **assassinations** are no longer unusual, but in 1963 the Kennedy shooting shocked the world. People cried in the street when they heard the news and it is said that everyone still remembers where they were and what they were doing when the news first reached them. Kennedy was a symbol of the youth culture and optimism of the United States and this helps explain the shock felt at his sudden death. Each year, 6 million people visit the JFK assassination site and a multi-million dollar tourism industry continues to thrive around what happened on one day in November 1963.

Who killed Kennedy?

The bare facts of the Kennedy assassination have led to a variety of **conspiracy theories** about who was behind the shooting. The generally accepted explanation is the one first put forward by the Warren Commission, a government enquiry. This concluded in 1964 that Oswald was acting alone when he shot Kennedy. The most popular alternative theory is that there was a second assassin, whom Oswald may or may not have known about, in front of Kennedy on the "Grassy Knoll." Nothing has ever been proved and the latest and most scientific re-examinations of the evidence all support the idea that Oswald was the sole gunman.

Texas Schoolbook Depository
Oswald's window
Warehouse
Records building
Criminal court and jail
Houston Street
Grassy Knoll
Elm Street

The arrow on this map shows the route President Kennedy's limousine took when he was assassinated in Dallas, Texas.

Racial injustice in South Africa

The modern country of South Africa was founded in the 19th century by the UK. The white settlers, or Afrikaners, were mostly descendants of the original Dutch **colonists**. The black population were not given the right to vote, even though they made up the overwhelming majority of the population. The white government brought in laws that treated blacks as inferior. This racist system was called **apartheid**, an Afrikaner word meaning "separateness." It forced black people to live in special "homelands" where the land was poor and it was harder to make a living by farming. In the cities, where black people were needed as cheap labour, they were crowded into special "townships."

Apartheid

While white people created a good standard of life for themselves, the majority of the population became second-class citizens. **Racial segregation** applied to schools, sport and all other aspects of life. Black people lived in poverty, lacked proper medical care, and were forced to make long journeys to find work. Special laws called pass laws restricted their right to travel and were very much resented.

Black people who protested against apartheid were accused of being **communists** and they faced severe punishment. They were not allowed to go on strike, but they formed a political party, the African National Congress (ANC).

On 21 March 1960, when a huge demonstration took place against the pass laws at the township of Sharpville, the police opened fire on protestors. Nearly 70 Africans were killed, thousands were arrested and beaten, and the ANC was banned.

Nelson Mandela

Up until Sharpville, the protest movement in South Africa had been non-violent. Faced with the violence of the authorities, the ANC decided to use violent methods of protest. A number of bomb attacks on government buldings followed and black leaders were arrested and imprisoned. One of these leaders was Nelson Mandela, who was imprisoned in 1962.

Sharpville

"The police opened fire; the officers emphasized that they had their backs to the wall, facing a frenzied mob of 20,000 natives."

(POLICE REPORT)

"There were not more than 5,000 Africans present; they were not carrying sticks or other arms and they had no violent intentions."

(A WOUNDED EYEWITNESS)

"The **post-mortem** examinations, which I made on 52 of the Africans, showed that 70 per cent of the bullets had entered from the back."

(REPORT FROM A SURGEON)

Nearly 70 Africans lie dead after police opened fire on the protestors in Sharpville, South Africa, 21 March 1960.

WAR AND POLITICS

The UK government faced its own problems of racism. The economy was strong and non-whites, from countries that were once part of the British **Empire**, were encouraged by the government to settle in the UK. Some British people, brought up to think of white culture as superior, had difficulty in accepting non-whites as equals. Racial prejudice became a part of life in the UK. Meanwhile the Cold War raged on.

Vietnam

The Cold War spread to the divided country of Vietnam in Asia. South Vietnam had a government friendly towards the United States, while North Vietnam had a communist government. The South would not hold elections, fearing the communists would win, and a **civil war** developed between the two halves of the country.

US leaders spoke of a "**domino effect**" in Asia. They meant that one communist country would help bring about the existence of another communist country, like dominoes knocking each other over, until the whole region "fell" to communism. President Kennedy supported South Vietnam, and gave the government money and thousands of military advisers. He was hoping to make sure the government stayed non-communist. However, more and more Vietnamese peasants began supporting the Viet Cong. This was the name given to the **guerrillas** fighting the South Vietnam government. In 1964, the United States claimed that North Vietnamese gunboats fired at US destroyers in the Gulf of Tonkin. The following year President Johnson, who took over as president after Kennedy was assassinated, ordered the bombing of North Vietnam. He hoped to weaken the communist government, and over half a million US troops were sent to South Vietnam to fight the Viet Cong.

A group of US troops jump from a helicopter on a mission to find the position of the enemy Viet Cong, 6 July 1967.

By 1968, the Viet Cong had widespread support from peasants, as well as military support from the communist governments of North Vietnam, China, and the USSR. In 1968, the US army was killing thousands of Viet Cong and their supporters each week. Despite this, the Viet Cong mounted a large-scale attack, called the Tet offensive, which gave them temporary control of three-quarters of South Vietnam. When Nixon became President in 1969, it was becoming clear that military victory by US forces was not likely to happen. There was no intention, however, to admit defeat and the grim war continued. Many adults in the United States supported the war in Vietnam, but a lot of young people, especially students, were against what was happening.

US troops in Vietnam

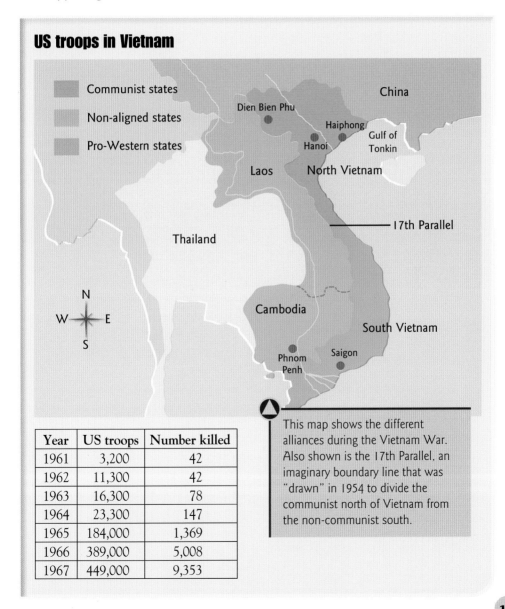

Year	US troops	Number killed
1961	3,200	42
1962	11,300	42
1963	16,300	78
1964	23,300	147
1965	184,000	1,369
1966	389,000	5,008
1967	449,000	9,353

This map shows the different alliances during the Vietnam War. Also shown is the 17th Parallel, an imaginary boundary line that was "drawn" in 1954 to divide the communist north of Vietnam from the non-communist south.

Israel and the Palestinians

In 1948, the country of **Israel** was established in Palestine. Two-thirds of the people in this territory in the **Middle East** were Palestinian Arabs, one-third were Israeli Jews. The creation of Israel immediately caused a war between Jews and Palestinians. Israel won this war, and this led to an enlargement of Israel. Around 600,000 Palestinians were expelled from Israel and Israeli-occupied land. They ended up in refugee camps in neighbouring Arab countries such as Jordan.

Background to war

The war that had broken out when Israel came into existence erupted once again in 1967, known as the Six-Day War because it lasted less than a week. Three Arab countries: Iraq, Syria, and Egypt, took the lead in opposing Israel. Along with Syria, Jordan and Lebanon began moving troops close to their borders with Israel.

The Israel-Arab conflict was also tied up with the Cold War between the United States and the USSR. Israel was supported by the United States because Israel wanted a US presence in the Middle East. The Middle East was the source of much of the oil that the prosperity of the West depended on. The USSR also wanted to increase its influence in the Middle East. It encouraged Egypt and Syria to be hostile to Israel and hinted they would help with arms if war broke out. The United States acted in the same way towards Israel.

The Six-Day War

By June 1967, Israel was facing the prospect of an attack from all sides. It decided to defend itself by attacking first, while the Arab armies were still organizing themselves and getting prepared. Israeli weapons destroyed most of Egypt's air force on the ground in Egypt. Israeli tanks then swept into and captured the Sinai, which belonged to Egypt, and occupied the Gaza Strip, the Palestinian land between Israel and Egypt. The west bank of the River Jordan and the Palestinian half of Jerusalem were taken from Jordan. On the last day of the Six-Day War, Israel attacked and captured the Golan Heights from Syria.

The map shows the changes in territory in the Middle East after the Six-Day War of 1967.

Living with the past

Some of the problems at the heart of the present-day conflict between Palestinians and Jews in the Middle East go back to the consequences of the Six-Day War of 1967. There were now almost 1 million Palestinians living under the rule of Israel and up to 400,000 Palestinians were turned into **refugees**, living in camps in Jordan and Lebanon. In the camps, armed guerrilla movements were formed, determined to regain the land they had lost in the War.

Who is to blame?

Historians do not agree about who was responsible for the Six-Day War.

- Some say the Cold War was to blame, with both the United States and the USSR seeking to gain influence in the Middle East.
- Some blame the **Arab countries**, especially Egypt, seeking to destroy Israel.
- Some blame Israel, seeking to enlarge its territory and knock out its enemies.

Egyptian soldiers lie on the floor as they surrender to the Israeli army during the Six-Day War, Gaza Strip, 1967.

The civil rights movement

Huge numbers of Civil Rights demonstrators gather around the Reflecting Pool at the Washington Monument, Washington, D.C., after their historic march of support for the Civil Rights Act.

In parts of the United States, especially the southern states, white people grew up thinking black people were inferior. Racial segregation existed in everyday life. In 1960, a **Civil Rights** Act helped African Americans register as voters but, as with other such laws, **discrimination** continued.

In August 1963, between 100,000 and 200,000 African Americans marched in Washington, D.C., in support of a Civil Rights Act. This would put an end to segregation. It was delayed from becoming law because some racist politicians were against it. Racial tensions were reaching a high point. Just a month after the Washington march, racists set off a bomb in a Birmingham, Alabama, church. As a result of this blast, four African-American girls were killed and over twenty people were injured. The Civil Rights Act finally became law in July 1964.

Struggling for equality

The Civil Rights Act met strong opposition in much of the South of the United States. Just days after the Civil Rights Act was signed, three civil rights workers (one black and two white) were found murdered in Mississippi. Two **Ku Klux Klan (KKK)** members and the local deputy sheriff were eventually found to be guilty. However, it was clear that the struggle for civil rights was not over. The tension was rising.

Getting angry

Martin Luther King led a non-violent protest for civil rights, but some black groups felt that they should use the same kind of violent methods that were being used against them. Groups such as the **Black Panthers** were formed in the 1960s, and some black leaders became Muslims because they felt that Christianity was the religion of white racists. At the same time, riots were breaking out in cities throughout the North.

Towards the end of 1965, it was revealed that 27 civil rights workers had been killed over the previous 5 years without anyone ever being convicted. In the summer of that year the anger of African Americans erupted in five days of rioting in the Watts area of Los Angeles. Around 30 people were killed, hundreds were injured, and 18,000 armed National Guards were brought in by the government to deal with the riot.

Members of the Black Panthers march in protest of the deaths of 27 civil rights workers, New York, 1966.

Slow progress

More laws were passed while Johnson was President. There was the **Voting Rights Act** in 1965 and, in 1968, another Civil Rights Act that made it illegal to sell or rent property to only one racial group. Progress was slow because of the time it took to change racist attitudes. African Americans continued to find it difficult to get work, let alone well-paid jobs. African Americans were equal in the eyes of the law, but in **economic** terms many remained second-class citizens.

Black pride

African Americans were angry at still being treated as second-class citizens. They stood up for themselves and this new energy and confidence was expressed in the soul music of the 1960s. It came from the soul, from the heart of people celebrating pride at being black. Ray Charles, Otis Redding and Aretha Franklin were leading soul singers but perhaps the greatest of all was James Brown. His big hits throughout the 1960s included "Say It Loud, I'm Black and I'm Proud." He came to own three radio stations, including one in Augusta, Georgia where he had once worked as a shoeshiner.

James Brown, "the Godfather of Soul," in an appearance on American television on the *Dick Cavett Show* in the 1960s.

Trouble in Northern Ireland

Most of Ireland, governed by the UK for centuries, achieved independence in January 1922. However, a part of the country remained tied to the UK and this led to violent conflict in 1968.

History is to blame

In the north of the island there were nine counties, called Ulster, where a minority of people wanted to remain part of the UK. Called **Unionists** – because they wanted union with the UK – they were descendants of **Protestants** who had settled there more than three centuries earlier. Most of the wealthier people in Ulster were Protestants and they feared they would lose their power in an independent Ireland. Protestants also feared they would be **discriminated** against because of their religion. This was because the Catholic Church had a lot of power in the rest of Ireland.

Northern Ireland was created out of six of the nine Ulster counties in 1921. The six – Fermanagh, Tyrone, Derry, Antrim, Armagh, and Down – were chosen because their total number of Protestants was larger than the total number of Catholics. Although Protestants were a minority in the nine Ulster counties put together, as they were in Ireland as a whole, in Northern Ireland they now made up a majority. Northern Ireland had its own **parliament** and the Protestant Unionists were able to use their majority to pass laws that discriminated against Catholics.

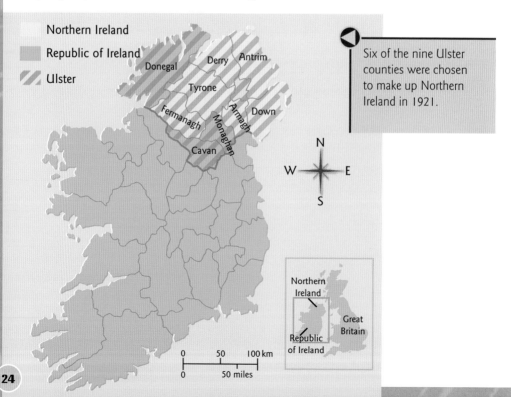

Six of the nine Ulster counties were chosen to make up Northern Ireland in 1921.

Protests and riots

When it came to finding employment, Catholics in Northern Ireland were treated as second-class citizens. They found it difficult to protest because the voting system prevented Catholics from getting elected as **councillors** and Members of Parliament. Many felt the same way as African Americans did in parts of the United States.

The civil rights movement in the United States inspired Catholics in Northern Ireland to organize a similar movement of their own. Their first march, in 1968, was attacked by Unionists. The police, a Protestant force, failed to protect them.

The following year there were more marches. Serious riots and street fighting broke out in Derry and Belfast. Unionist gangs attacked Catholic areas and houses were set on fire. Catholics began fleeing across the border to the Republic of Ireland. As they passed through Protestant areas, gangs stoned trains carrying the Catholic refugees. Troops from the Republic of Ireland were sent to the border because it seemed they might have to cross into Northern Ireland to protect the Catholics.

Civil rights protestors march in London. The Northern Irish Catholics' banner reads "We demand democracy in Northern Ireland."

The UK government sent troops into Northern Ireland to try to calm the situation. At first they were welcomed by the Catholics, but this feeling soon changed when they felt that the army was not acting fairly. Most Catholics were **Nationalists** and wanted a united Ireland. The troops came to be seen as being on the side of the Unionists and against the Catholics. The Irish Republican Army (IRA), which had developed out of Ireland's earlier struggle for independence, had fallen into decline but now it grew stronger. It acted as a force defending Catholics and as a guerrilla army opposed to the UK. What followed was 30 years of conflict and bloodshed.

A divided state

Catholics and Protestants went to different schools and lived in different neighbourhoods. They grew up thinking the worst of each other. Two different flags were hoisted throughout residential areas. The Protestant Unionists flew the Union Jack (UK flag) or Northern Irish flag, while the Catholics flew the Irish Tricolour. This ensured that everyone who visited knew who controlled the area.

THE END OF AN ERA

The optimism of the 1960s in the UK seemed to reach a peak when the England football team won the World Cup in 1966. There was also a sense that people should be given more control over their lives. Divorce was made a lot easier and abortion was made legal in 1967. Two years later, parliament abolished the death penalty. Other developments seemed to spell trouble. In 1968, Enoch Powell, a Conservative politician, predicted "rivers of blood" unless **immigration** was halted. This stirred up bad feelings and made some people afraid of more immigrants settling in the UK.

Almost a French revolution

In May 1968, French students organized large protests against the authority of their universities in Paris. On the evening of 10 May the students built barricades in part of the city. When the police moved in, a riot developed. Days later, a protest against police violence led to half a million people marching in the streets of Paris. Then factory workers joined them, going on strike, occupying factories, and making their own demands for better pay and shorter hours of work.

By 20 May, around 2 million French workers were on strike and 120 factories were occupied. Some days later the **Stock Exchange** in Paris was burned down. It began to seem as if a revolution might occur. Then, **trade union** leaders made a deal accepting wage increases, and the strikes were called off.

Students stand against French police in a Paris street during the riots of May 1968.

Protests

What happened in France was exceptional, but in the same year there were a number of demonstrations around the world. There was widespread anger about the United States' involvement in the war in Vietnam and in 1968 a large protest took place in London. There were also anti-war protests in Australia, which had sent troops to Vietnam in 1965. In 1967, Muhammad Ali, the world heavy-weight boxing champion, had his title taken away because he refused to fight in Vietnam.

The Prague Spring

Czechoslovakia in Eastern Europe was under the control of the USSR, but in 1968 Dubcek became the new leader of the Czech government. Dubcek was still a communist, but he and his supporters wanted the government to interfere less in people's lives. The USSR was worried that this might weaken their power in eastern Europe and in August they invaded Czechoslovakia. Faced with Soviet tanks and soldiers in Prague, the capital city, Dubcek was forced to resign. This brief time when Czech society had become more free, with a communist government more willing to listen to what people wanted, became known as the Prague Spring. It failed and traditional communism, under the authority of the USSR, was restored.

Soviet tanks line a Prague street with their guns facing at Radio Prague. People had gathered there to hear the latest news about the Soviet invasion of 1968.

"The times they are a-changin' "

One way in which the times were changing as the 1960s drew to a close was the feeling that violence was becoming a part of everyday life, not just something that happened in faraway, foreign countries.

In April 1968, Martin Luther King was assassinated by James Earl Ray, a white racist, while standing on the balcony of a motel in Memphis. The following month Robert Kennedy, a brother of the assassinated president, was shot dead. In 1969, the actress Sharon Tate, along with a group of her friends, was murdered by Charles Manson and his followers. The time when politicians and public figures needed to be surrounded by bodyguards had arrived.

Anti-war

The times were also changing as, across the United States and Europe, protests continued against the Vietnam War. By April 1969, over 33,000 Americans had lost their lives in Vietnam and some people were questioning the reasons for the war. The **compulsory** calling-up of young men for service in Vietnam, called the draft, became very unpopular. Student protests against the war increased, but the fighting went on.

In 1969, John Lennon returned an award medal that he and the other Beatles had received from the Queen. He criticised the British monarchy as "snobbery and part of the class system" and said that he regretted accepting the medal. He was returning it, he announced, as a protest against war.

Anti-Vietnam protestors march towards a rally at the Washington Monument, United States. They carry banners that plead "End the war in Vietnam now!"

END THE WAR IN VIETNAM NOW

Hippies

Many young people in the West began to criticise their society. It became fashionable to dress and behave in a way that represented a different way of thinking. The term hippy came to describe young people who grew their hair long, wore colourful **ethnic** clothes, and spoke of "dropping out" of society.

For the first time, young people – and not just the rich – began to travel abroad and experience other cultures. Hippies praised societies that tried to avoid war and did not keep spending money on material goods. They tried to live by their beliefs and set up communes. People living in communes shared everything they owned. In the United States, parts of the city of San Francisco, California, became famous as a centre for hippy communities.

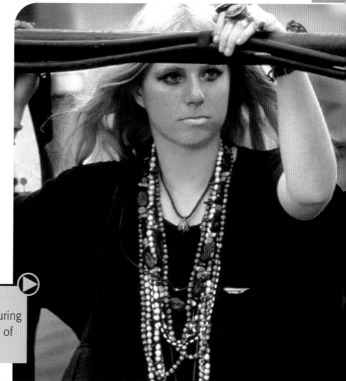

A young festival-goer wears strings of beads and bells and flowing clothes during the Woodstock Music and Art Festival of August 1969.

Haight-Ashbury and "The Summer of Love"

In the mid 1960s, Haight-Ashbury, a neighbourhood in San Francisco, California, flourished into a centre for the "love and peace" message of the hippie movement. Haight-Ashbury's music scene was thriving, with hundreds of free rock concerts held either outdoors, or in huge ballrooms such as The Fillmore and The Avalon. Bands such as The Grateful Dead, Jefferson Airplane, and Quicksilver Messenger Service performed experimental music against a backdrop of **psychedelic** light shows.

During the summer of 1967, which was nick-named "The Summer of Love", thousands of teenagers flocked to the area to experience the alternative music, fashions, and lifestyle of the hippies. However, the Haight-Ashbury scene ended just as quickly as it had started. Many of the first generation hippies resented the commercial nature that the movement had now taken on. As 1967 drew to a close, many of the original Haight-Ashbury hippies had already left the San Francisco area and had moved to the northwestern regions of the United States. However, the hippie movement continued to attract huge numbers of followers for the rest of the 1960s, and peaked with the Woodstock Festival of 1969 (see pages 30–31).

The end of the sixties

After the end of the Second World War there was an increase in the birth rate. This **baby boom** produced the young people who came of age during the 1960s. They formed new beliefs and the attitude that people could question their government and protest for causes they believed in. This outlook on life was radically different to their parents who had grown up in hard times and lived through a world war. Compared to them, the Beatles fans, the hippies, and the students who marched in the streets had grown up in prosperity and peace. Many were mainly interested in personal freedom and "doing their own thing." Many others began to question and challenge the politics that their parents had learnt to accept. Some hippies offered flowers as a symbol of peace and love, but others campaigned for social and political change.

Achievements

As well as the rights gained by African Americans, advances were also made by women – who demanded equal pay. They began to question old-fashioned attitudes that treated them as inferior and weaker than men.

The optimism and the sense of achievement of the sixties were captured in two events of 1969. On 21 July, Neil Armstrong was one of three US astronauts to reach the Moon. Armstrong was the first to step foot outside the landing craft, and he broadcast back to Earth the message: "That's one small step for man, one giant leap for mankind." The other event, the Woodstock Music and Art Festival, took place less than a month after the Moon landing. About 400,000 people turned up at Bethel Sullivan County, New York, for a huge music festival. The festival was staged for three days. The organizers hadn't planned on so many people turning up. It was overcrowded, there was little food, and the surrounding roads were jammed with traffic. But, there was no violence reported at all, and the Woodstock Festival represented the high point of the "hippie" era.

Jimi Hendrix, one of the most talented guitarists ever to have lived, plays at the Woodstock music festival in 1969.

The sixties, however, was also a period of violence and war. Another rock music festival, in December 1969, came to represent the end of the "swinging sixties." The festival was in the United States at Altamont, California. The Rolling Stones hired a motorcycle gang, called the Hells Angels, to manage security around the stage. It was not a wise decision because the Hells Angels acted aggressively towards fans. One fan, perhaps under the influence of drugs, drew a weapon and was attacked and killed by one of the Hells Angels. The Rolling Stones, along with the audience watching them, were shocked that such a violent event could happen at a supposedly peaceful rock festival. The peace and love dream of the hippy sixties was over. The murder at Altamont came to represent the nature of violence in the world that ended the hippy dream.

Artists who performed at Woodstock

The albums of many of the singers and bands that performed at Woodstock are still available and highly regarded by music critics. They include:

Arlo Guthrie	Jeff Beck Group
The Band	Jefferson Airplane
Blood, Sweat & Tears	Jimi Hendrix
Creedence Clearwater Revival	Joan Baez
Crosby, Stills & Nash (and Young)	Joe Cocker
Sly and the Family Stone	Johnny Winter
Grateful Dead	Ravi Shankar
Incredible String Band	Santana
Janis Joplin	The Who

The Rolling Stones play at the Altamont Rock festival in December 1969. The Hells Angels, hired as security, are pictured on the left.

THE 1970s

The Conservatives formed a new UK government in 1970. They had a different approach to running the country from the previous Labour government. They decided that spending cuts had to be made in order to improve the economy and make everyone better off. Free milk to primary school children was abolished and, for the first time, museums and art galleries introduced admission charges. In 1971, a crowd of 100,000 people filled Trafalgar Square in a protest against proposals for a new law, limiting the right of workers to go on strike. The early 1970s was a period of unrest as conflicts between trade unionists and the government grew.

A dark decade

Compared to the sense of optimism of the 1960s, the 1970s seemed a more cynical and hopeless decade. There was no sudden break between the mood of the end of the 1960s and the beginning of the 1970s. What happened instead, was that unfinished conflicts from the 1960s rose violently to the surface in the 1970s. What seemed like fresh problems, in places like Northern Ireland and the Middle East, were really old ones that had never been settled.

Kent State

In 1970, US President Nixon announced that US troops had invaded Cambodia, a country bordering Vietnam, because it was being used by the Viet Cong to transport supplies. This produced larger anti-war protests in the United States than ever before. At Kent State University in Ohio, national guardsmen opened fire on a student protest and four students were killed. The killing of innocent students added to the feeling that the hippy attitude of the sixties was over.

National guardsmen fire tear gas at students on campus at Kent State University in Ohio, United States.

Hijacks

In the Middle East, a guerrilla force within the **Palestine Liberation Organization (PLO)** began hijacking planes. This was an attempt to force Israel to release Palestinian prisoners. One hijack ended in failure when the crew overcame the hijackers but three other planes were successfully hijacked the same day – 6 September 1970. One landed in Egypt and was blown up on the runway after the passengers were allowed to leave. Two others landed in Jordan where they were soon joined by another plane that had been hijacked later. Most of the passengers were released, some were taken hostage and were released just before the planes were blown up the next day on the runway .

Jordan, which had a lot of Palestinian refugees, was frightened at being blamed for what had happened. It decided to take action against the Palestinian refugees. Fighting broke out and thousands died.

Piracy in the air

"Four hijacks over Western Europe made yesterday the worst day for terrorism in the history of civil aviation. Three succeeded and the other failed after a hijacker was shot dead in a battle over the North Sea. Palestinian guerrillas have claimed credit for the attacks."

(FROM THE TIMES, 7 SEPTEMBER 1970)

Terrorists blow up one of three hijacked airplanes on the runway in Egypt, 6 September 1970.

Signs of the times

Some events in the early years of the 1970s showed how society was changing. In 1970, London was the setting for the annual Miss World beauty contest but this time there were dramatic protests. Women demonstrators disrupted the ceremony, throwing rotten fruit and stink bombs. They accused the show of degrading women by parading them in bikinis, as if they were exhibits at a flower or dog show. It was time, said the protestors, for women to be freed from a male-dominated world that treated them as inferior.

Imprisoned without trial

After the arrival of UK troops in Northern Ireland, the IRA began to gather support from a section of the Catholic population. What had started out as a campaign for civil rights developed into a struggle for a united Ireland. A guerrilla war developed as fighting broke out between the IRA and the UK army. In 1971, the UK government allowed for people suspected of being in the IRA to be arrested and imprisoned without a trial. This caused further resentment and the guerrilla war got worse.

The microchip arrives

In 1971, a United States company, Intel Corporation, announced it had developed the first **microprocessor**. This used silicon, a material that allowed electronic circuits to be printed on a tiny **chip** measuring just over half a centimetre (a quarter of an inch) square. The power of computers, which until then had been large, bulky machines, could now be reduced to a system small enough to fit on an office desk. Silicon chips could be cheaply produced and this meant computers would be affordable to businesses. By 1970, pocket calculators went on sale in the United States. It was claimed that it would only be a matter of time before ordinary people had computers in their homes.

Hot pants

The miniskirt had disappeared in the late sixties and fashion designers returned to below-the-knee hemlines and traditional suits for women. Young people rejected this by wearing "hot pants," which were ultra-short and were worn mainly by women.

The pop singer Lulu poses in hot pants and knee-length boots in London in the 1970s.

Glam rock and disco

In the early 1970s, a new kind of music began to emerge that would come to be called glam rock. It was partly a reaction against the more serious and hippy kind of rock music that groups such as Pink Floyd had explored. Glam rock began in Britain with Roxy Music and their singer Bryan Ferry, and it became very influential. It was marked by outrageous and colourful clothing and hairstyles – very different to the often unkempt hippie styles.

In the United States, the new kind of music becoming popular was called disco music. It was up-tempo music played at first for dancers in nightclubs rather than for listeners of the radio and records. It became hugely influential. Funk music also became more popular, and its audience was now more diverse than its original, mostly black, audiences. In 1971, funk music reached an even wider audience with Isaac Hayes' soundtrack for the film *Shaft*.

Glam rock band Roxy Music (shown here in 1973) became famous for the glamorous fashion style that accompanied their music.

1972 – a violent year

Various unfinished conflicts from around the world reached violent climaxes in 1972 and shocked the general public.

Bloody Sunday

On Sunday 30 January, the civil rights movement in Northern Ireland organized a march through the streets of Derry. This was to protest about the inequalities still affecting the Catholic population. The UK army, patrolling the event, opened fire on the protestors and killed thirteen people. The army claimed they had been fired on first, but all those killed were civilians. Some were shot in the back, and there was no evidence to support the army. The effect of Bloody Sunday, as it was called, was to multiply support for the IRA and increase the violence from all sides in the conflict.

A huge crowd of Protestants gather to protest against the Bloody Sunday massacre in Derry, Northern Ireland.

"I couldn't believe it"

Sean Collins was nine years old on Bloody Sunday and he watched the civil rights march coming down the street where he lived:

"What I saw next after that I couldn't believe, not really at first at all. An army troop carrier appeared, and it started coming slowly towards us down the street. Then the troop carrier stopped, and out of it, or from another one that had just come along by its side, half a dozen soldiers jumped out. They stood by the vehicle a minute: and then slowly and deliberately each one of them went down on his knees and started to fire steadily into the crowd. It was like as if they were doing a sort of training demonstration, that's the only way I can describe it."

(FROM *HOW IT HAPPENED* EDITED BY JON E. LEWIS)

Massacre at Munich

The fighting between Jordan and the Palestinians in 1970 ended with the Palestine Liberation Organization (PLO), the main group representing the Palestinians, agreeing to leave Jordan. This did not solve the problem of the Palestinians who had no country to call their own and who had lost land to Israel. Palestinian guerrillas decided to take their armed struggle to the West, which they believed was supporting Israel. At the Olympic Games in Munich, Germany, in 1972, they took eleven Israeli athletes hostage, demanding the release of imprisoned Palestinians. Israel refused. The German police tried to rescue the hostages but they were all killed. The Middle East conflict continued.

Armed police drop into position directly above the apartment where 26 members of the Israeli Olympic team were being held hostage.

Vietnam – war goes on

The United States wanted to leave Vietnam, but this was difficult to do without admitting to defeat. The Viet Cong launched a large-scale attack in April 1972 and President Nixon ordered the bombing of civilian and military targets in North Vietnam. Protests continued in the United States and the US government began talks to arrange a **ceasefire** with North Vietnam and pull out all of its troops.

The rise of Nixon

While US President John F. Kennedy had the looks of a film star and an attractive personality, Richard Nixon, by comparison, looked rather ordinary and glum. Nevertheless, as the **Republican** candidate for president of the United States in the 1960 election, he only lost to Kennedy by a very narrow margin.

Nixon and Vietnam

At the time of the 1968 elections for president, there was much social and political unrest in the United States due to the civil rights movement and the Vietnam War. Nixon stood as a politician appealing to older, white voters who were troubled by all this unrest. He narrowly won the election and became president.

Nixon wanted US forces out of Vietnam, but he also wanted to stop North Vietnam from claiming victory. The South Vietnamese army was given support and training so that it could take over from the United States in fighting the Viet Cong. At the same time Nixon began talks with the government of North Vietnam, hoping to secure a ceasefire before the US presidential elections of 1972. Nixon had established friendly relations with China, and the Chinese government were putting pressure on North Vietnam to make a deal with the United States. US diplomacy was combined with heavy bombing raids on North Vietnam. Many civilians were killed but Nixon wanted to appear powerful so as to strengthen his bargaining position when it came to talking about a ceasefire.

In the 1972 elections for US president, Nixon portrayed himself as a peacemaker. He claimed he could get the United States out of the war without surrendering. He said that an agreement with North Vietnam was almost final. This worked well with voters and Nixon was re-elected as president, this time by a landslide victory.

President Nixon and Vice-President Spiro Agnew wave to supporters at the victory rally, after securing a landslide victory in the election of 1972.

Keeping secrets

Nixon liked to keep secrets. The bombing of Laos and Cambodia that he ordered in 1970 was kept secret from the American people. Nixon also wanted to weaken the anti-war movement so he ordered the phone lines of anti-war leaders to be secretly tapped. He also gave his authority for the offices of anti-war groups to be burgled in order to collect information on the anti-war movement.

In June 1972, in the run up to the presidential elections, five burglars were caught trying to enter office rooms in the Watergate building, headquarters of the **Democratic** Party in Washington. At the time, no one connected this event with Nixon and his secret operations against those who opposed him.

A divided country

Nixon's part in the Vietnam War and the attitude to anti-war protestors in the United States divided the people of the country:

Nixon, himself, described anti-war demonstrators as "bums."

A government investigation into the killing of four students at an anti-war protest at Kent State University said that: "A nation that uses weapons of war upon its youth is a nation on the edge of chaos."

Thousands of student protestors demonstrate against the Vietnam War, chanting "Nixon, assassin!"

Endings and beginnings

The talks between the United States and North Vietnam did not produce the ceasefire as quickly as Nixon had claimed they would in the US presidential elections. In twelve days over Christmas 1972, North Vietnam was bombed more heavily than ever before. Events in Chile were also causing problems for the United States.

Ending the Vietnam War

Finally, early in 1973, an agreement was signed between the United States and North Vietnam. US troops were to be withdrawn from Vietnam and US prisoners of war would be released. Viet Cong troops would be allowed to remain in South Vietnam but fighting would stop. This did not please members of the government of South Vietnam because the Viet Cong did not support them. Nixon promised to continue supporting South Vietnam if fighting started up again.

Nixon claimed he had ended the Vietnam War and brought "peace with honour." US troops left, but the war was not really over because the problem of Vietnam being split into two parts had not been solved. When the war started again in 1973, Nixon's promise of support came to nothing and, by 1975, Vietnam was finally united as one country. North Vietnamese forces took over South Vietnam and the last helicopters carrying US and pro-US Vietnamese took off from the US embassy in Saigon, the capital of South Vietnam, in April 1975.

Fleeing US troops board a US Marine helicopter at an airbase in Saigon, South Vietnam, after troops from communist North Vietnam invade the South in 1975.

Beginning trouble in Chile

Many of the countries in South America were controlled by a group of rich people at the expense of the poor. In 1970, the people of Chile elected a new government that promised to share the country's wealth more equally. Salvador Allende became the president and, supported by communists and **socialists**, he began a series of **reforms**.

The United States did not want Allende in power because the success of a socialist government in one country in South America might encourage other countries in the region to elect similar governments. Cuba was already enough of a problem and having the two socialist countries – Chile and Cuba – nearby was seen as too much of a threat to the non-communist business interests of the United States. Years later, when the United States admitted to supporting the overthrow of Allende, it blamed the Cold War for creating the fear that Chile would become a base for anti-American activities.

Armed guards keep a lookout for attackers as the Chilean President, Salvador Allende, leaves a building during the military overthrow in 1973.

Allende had been elected by the people of Chile, so Nixon could not openly use force to remove him. Instead, the United States made sure that Chile did not receive bank loans from anyone and the country's economy grew very weak as a result. Money was given to Allende's opponents and in 1973 the government was overthrown and military leaders took control of Chile. Supporters of Allende were tortured and killed and trade unions were abolished. A **dictatorship** friendly to the United States was established, led by General Pinochet. Fifty years of **democracy** in Chile came to a violent end.

The human cost of the Vietnam War

Groups in Vietnam	Killed
US soldiers	58,000
South Vietnamese soldiers	224,000
South Vietnamese civilians	2 million
North Vietnamese soldiers	1.1 million
North Vietnamese civilians	2 million
Other nationalities	5,300
Total estimated death toll	**5.4 million**

Israel-Arab war – again

After their defeat in the Six-Day War of 1967, Arab countries in the Middle East had to decide what to do about Israel and the homeless Palestinians. Jordan had expelled the Palestinian Liberation Organization (PLO) and withdrawn from the conflict. Egypt wanted to negotiate with Israel and regain its territory, the Sinai, which had been lost to Israel. Syria, with some of its territory also under Israeli occupation, wanted a military solution and prepared for another war.

Surprise attack

Israel wanted to keep the Sinai and rejected Egypt's attempt to negotiate. Egypt then decided to team up with Syria and attack Israel, thinking this would force Israel to negotiate. In October 1973, Egypt and Syria launched an attack on Israel that took them by complete surprise.

Israel was almost defeated in the war, but the United States helped with a massive airlift of military equipment. The Arab forces, supplied by the USSR, were driven back. When the war ended Israel's borders remained as they were, but the country had been shaken by the Arab show of strength. Egypt and Israel did begin to talk and eventually a settlement was reached. The Sinai was returned to Egypt and Egypt withdrew from the conflict. Syria, with its territory of the Golan Heights still under Israeli occupation, did not make peace with Israel. The conflict went on, the Palestinians remained homeless, and it was only a matter of time before more fighting would break out.

A bomb explodes in the distance as troops look on in surprise during the Israel-Arab conflict of October 1973.

Holding back the oil

Arab countries realized they could control the amount of oil that was sold to the West. In 1973, they reduced the supply of oil and doubled its price, demanding that Israel return to the borders that existed before the 1967 Six-Day War. This produced shortages of oil in Europe and plans were drawn up for the **rationing** of petrol. By the beginning of 1974 talks with the Arab countries restored the supply of oil. What was brought home to many people was the fact that the West's way of life depended on the supply of Middle East oil.

The lights go out

Oil is used to produce electricity as well, so winter 1973 did not see the usual display of Christmas lights in the capitals of western European cities. West Germany introduced petrol rationing, and driving on Sundays was made illegal. The main roads on Sundays were taken over by cyclists, walkers, and horse-riders. Anyone driving a car without a good excuse was fined on the spot and the police reported a sudden increase in the theft of petrol from parked cars.

The roads of West Germany are completely empty on a Sunday in the winter of 1973.

TRIUMPH AND FAILURE

There were occasions to celebrate in the UK in the early 1970s. Hundreds of thousands of young people turned up to a summer music festival on the Isle of Wight. It seemed as if the hippy spirit of the sixties had not completely died out. Not everyone was happy, though, and local people complained about the loud music that disturbed them for the week long "festival of music and love."

Muhammad Ali – champion of the world

In 1964, a young American boxer changed his name to Muhammad Ali. He was publicly rejecting the name he was born with in 1942, Cassius Clay, as a "slave name." As an African American from the southern US state of Kentucky, Ali knew that slavery had been abolished but that racial discrimination still existed. As a talented boxer, he claimed he was "the Greatest" and in 1964 he proved this by beating Sonny Liston and becoming heavyweight champion of the world. He went on to successfully defend his title nine times from 1965 to 1967.

The civil rights movement overlapped with the movement against the Vietnam War, with people pointing out that while African Americans made up only 11 per cent of the United States' population, more than twice that percentage of the soldiers in Vietnam were African American. Ali refused to join the military and fight in Vietnam, saying, "I ain't got no quarrel with the Viet Cong," and in 1967 he was stripped of his boxing title and barred from the boxing ring because of this. Ali had the courage to stand up for what he believed in even though it cost him a great deal.

This young American boxer, Muhammad Ali, would become world-famous for his supreme strength and talent in the boxing ring.

Ali returned to the boxing ring in 1970, but he was not at the top of his form and lost a championship fight against Joe Frazier. He regained his form and defeated Frazier in January 1974. He then fought the reigning champion, George Foreman, in October of the same year. The fight took place in Kinshasa, Zaire, and was billed as the "rumble in the jungle." Ali knocked out Foreman and became the heavyweight champion of the world for the second time. His famous boast, that he could "float like a butterfly, sting like a bee" was justified because of the way he fought. He danced around the ring, sometimes taunting his opponent with his arms dangling at his side, but he was always ready to defend himself, or land a skilful blow at the right time.

Ali is regarded as the fastest, and most skilful, heavyweight boxing champion of all time. He became a hero to millions of people who admired his courage in taking a stand over the Vietnam War and then coming back to regain his title. His humour and his skill as a boxer were also admired and his victory in Zaire in 1974 was greeted with joy around the world. It was certainly the sporting triumph of the year and one of the great sporting achievements of the 20th century.

Sporting firsts

During the Olympic Games in Mexico, 1968, Americans Tommy Smith and John Carlos won gold and silver in the 200 metres. They wore black gloves and gave a Black Panther salute. South Africa was banned from taking part in the Olympics because of its policy of apartheid.

In the Football World Cup, held in Mexico, in 1970, Brazil beat Italy 4-1 in a thrilling final, and the Brazilian Pele proved he was the best footballer in the world.

US sprinters Tommy Smith and John Carlos raise their fists in the Black Panther salute on the podium of the 1968 Mexico Olympic Games.

Watergate

In 1972, when burglars were caught trying to enter the Democrats' office in the Watergate building in Washington, it turned out they were planning to repair bugging equipment that had been installed earlier. The purpose was to overhear private conversations between Democrats.

Scandal?

The following year, when those who had broken in to the Watergate building were on trial for their offence, two Washington journalists, called Carl Bernstein and Bob Woodward, became convinced that the five men had been acting for powerful people in the rival Republican Party. Was it possible that Nixon, the Republican politician recently re-elected as president, was involved in the Watergate break-in? If true, it would be the biggest political scandal of the century.

Watergate was such a huge event that a 1976 film, called *All the President's Men*, recounted the scandal. It starred Dustin Hoffmann and Robert Redford as Bernstein and Woodward, the journalists who had pieced together the story of President Nixon's involvement in the break-in.

Nixon's tapes

A special Investigating Committee was set up to find the truth and its proceedings were shown on television. It discovered that Nixon tape-recorded his conversations with other politicians in the White House. These tapes might reveal if he had been involved in the break-in at the Watergate building. When Nixon refused to hand over the tapes to the committee, people began to get suspicious. Later, some of the tapes were handed over, but sections had been erased. Some senior White House politicians were charged with a criminal offence for doing this, but was the President himself guilty?

Guilty

Nixon protested that he was innocent. He claimed that people working for him had acted illegally without his knowledge. He handed over printed versions of other taped White House conversations, called transcripts, to show he was not involved. Other people, however, showed that the transcripts did not cover all the conversations that had been taped, including a vital one about the Watergate break-in.

Through the summer of 1974, the case against Nixon grew. He was forced by the Supreme Court, the highest court in the United States, to hand over the other tapes. His connection with the Watergate break-in could not be proved definitely by these tapes, but to many people he was guilty. By August, even members of Nixon's own party were deserting him.

President Nixon was facing an almost certain **impeachment** trial and possible removal from office. Finally, on 8 August 1974, Nixon resigned in disgrace – the first US president ever to have stepped down. Other politicians involved also resigned, and some were sent to prison.

Nixon's resignation

In his resignation speech to the nation, Nixon said: "I have never been a quitter…but as President, I must put the interest of America first." Referring to Vietnam, he also reminded people how he and his government "have ended America's longest war" and how "we have unlocked the doors that for a quarter of a century stood between the United States and the People's Republic of China." Did his achievements outweigh his disgrace?

President Nixon gives his farewell speech at the White House in August 1974, after his involvement in the Watergate break-in came to light.

47

From Beatlemania to Watergate

In some respects the world had not changed enormously between the early 1960s and the mid 1970s. Poverty still affected many parts of the world, especially Africa, while most people in the West enjoyed a reasonably comfortable lifestyle. Some of the major problems facing the world in 1975, such as the Cold War, the Israeli-Arab conflict and the plight of the homeless Palestinians, had existed fifteen years earlier.

A different world

In other ways, though, the world had changed tremendously. One US president had been assassinated and another one had been forced to resign. What had begun as a small war in a faraway part of Asia, Vietnam, had turned into a major conflict and divided the US nation. The United State's civil rights movement had inspired protestors in other parts of the world, especially in Northern Ireland where it was met with fierce resistance and turned into a war. The protests and demonstrations and the violence that marked 1968 in different parts of the world did not belong to the world of Beatlemania and pop art.

The world of Watergate was not the world of hippies and peace and love. It was a world where a president could be involved in criminal activities, where aeroplanes could be hijacked and blown up and a world where satellites could beam pictures of what was happening across the globe and into the living rooms of millions of people. It was a world where people calling for civil rights could be killed.

The Beatles began as four young musicians wearing simple black suits and their early songs were uncomplicated. Their live performances needed a few amplifiers, but not a great deal more. By the time of Watergate, the Beatles had been split up for four years and the two main songwriters, John Lennon and Paul McCartney, had quarrelled and grown apart from each other. (However, they had all had success with solo records.)

John Lennon and his wife Yoko Ono speak during a press conference in New York, 1973.

Rock and roll with lipstick

"I once asked Lennon what he thought of what I do. He said 'It's great, but it's just rock'n'roll with lipstick on.' "

(DAVID BOWIE)

David Bowie

If The Beatles summed up the innocent spirit of the early sixties, David Bowie and his brand of glam rock summed up the very different spirit of the 1970s. His live performances were spectacular and dramatic, and so was his appearance. He wore make-up, dyed his hair orange, and dressed in clothes that were deliberately feminine. He invented a different character for each of his albums and went on world tours. It was an age when a lot of people found an escape from the real world in rock and roll stars that offered fantasy. When ex-Beatle John Lennon released an album in 1972, *Some Time In New York City*, with songs about Northern Ireland, racism in the United States, and the position of women in society, it made very little impact. The songs were too much about the real world.

British pop star David Bowie wears his trademark outrageous clothing and make-up, during the 1970s.

TIMELINE

1948
Creation of Israel

1959
A group of Cuban revolutionaries, led by Fidel Castro, take power in Cuba and the former dictator is forced to leave the country

1960
At Sharpville in South Africa, nearly 70 black protestors are shot dead by the police

1961
The US government gives support to an attempted invasion of Cuba

1962
Nelson Mandela imprisoned in South Africa
Cuban missile crisis

1963
President John F. Kennedy is assassinated in Dallas, Texas
The Beatles "Please Please Me" reaches the top of the UK music charts

1964
The Gulf of Tonkin incident in Vietnam
The boxer Cassius Clay changes his name to Muhammed Ali
The Beatles make their first tour of the United States
Muhammed Ali is heavyweight boxing champion of the world

1965
US President Lyndon B. Johnson orders the bombing of North Vietnam
The Voting Rights Act protects African Americans' right to vote in some southern US states

1966
In San Francisco, The Beatles perform for the last time on stage
England win the Football World Cup

1967
The Six-Day War ends in victory for Israel
Muhammad Ali, world heavyweight boxing champion, has his title taken away because he refuses to fight in Vietnam

1968

The Viet Cong Tet offensive

Anti-Vietnam War protests take place in the United States, UK, and Australia

Martin Luther King assassinated

Robert Kennedy assassinated

First Civil Rights march in Northern Ireland protesting against anti-Catholic discrimination

In Czechoslovakia, Dubcek becomes the new leader of the Czech government

1969

Danger of civil war in Northern Ireland leads to the UK government sending in troops

Richard M. Nixon becomes president of the United States

In July, three American astronauts land on the Moon

Woodstock music festival attracts 400,000 people

1970

The Beatles split up

Four students shot and killed by National Guardsmen at Kent State University

The Palestinian Liberation Organization hijacks aeroplanes

Bands such as Roxy Music introduce Glam rock

Democratic elections in Chile return Allende as president, promising a socialist government

In the Football World Cup, Brazil beat Italy 4–1

1971

UK troops kill thirteen civil rights protestors in Derry, Northern Ireland in what becomes known as Bloody Sunday

1972

The PLO take eleven Israeli athletes hostage at the Olympic Games

The Viet Cong launch a large-scale attack in South Vietnam

Richard Nixon, promising an end to the Vietnam War, is re-elected president

Five burglars are caught trying to enter the Watergate building

1973

Peace terms agreed between North Vietnam and the United States

With US support, Allende's socialist government is overthrown in Chile and a military dictator takes over

Surprise attack by Egypt and Syria on Israel backfires

1974

Muhammed Ali wins the world heavyweight boxing championship for the second time

Richard Nixon resigns in disgrace

1975

North Vietnamese troops overrun South Vietnam, and Vietnam is united as one independent country

FURTHER INFORMATION

CDs

Eyewitness: The 1960s (BBC Audiobooks, 2004)
Eyewitness: The 1970s (BBC Audiobooks, 2004)

Books

American Women of the Vietnam War, Amanda Ferguson (Rosen, 2004)
Leading Lives: Ho Chi Minh, David Downing (Heinemann Library, 2003)
The Assassination of John F. Kennedy, Lauren Spencer (Rosen, 2002)
The Assassination of Martin Luther King, Jacqueline Ching (Rosen, 2002)
The Cuban Missile Crisis in American History, Paul Brubaker (Enslow, 2001)
The Little Rock School Desegregation Crisis in American History, Robert Somerlott (Enslow, 2001)
The Vietnam War: What are we Fighting For?, Deborah Kent (Enslow, 2001)
20th Century Design: The 60s: The Plastic Age, Julia Bigham (Heinemann Library, 1999)
20th Century Media: The 1960s: The Satellite Age, Steve Parker (Heinemann Library, 2002)
20th Century Music: The 1960s: The Age of Rock, Jackie Gaff (Heinemann Library, 2002)
Turning Points in History: The Moon Landing, Richard Tames (Heinemann Library, 2000)

Websites

http://en.wikipedia.org/wiki/1900s
Encyclopedia with sections on the 1900s and the 1910s

www.geocities.com/historygateway/1900.html
Weblinks to interesting sites relevant to the history of women in the UK

http://kclibrary.nhmccd.edu/decades.html
A history site of United States cultural history on a decade-by-decade basis

Disclaimer

All the internet addresses (URLs) given in this book were valid at the time of going to press. However, due to the dynamic nature of the Internet, some addresses may have changed, or sites may have ceased to exist since publication. While the author and publishers regret any inconvenience this may cause readers, no responsibility for any such changes can be accepted by either the author or the publishers.

the mid 1960s to the early 1970s

Books and literature	• *Jonathan Livingston Seagull* by Richard Bach (1970) • *Watership Down* by Richard Adams (1972) • *All the President's Men* by Carl Bernstein and Bob Woodward (1974)
Fads and fashions	• G.I. Joe, made by Hasbro, is the first action figure for boys • The electronic pocket calculator is invented in 1971
Historic events	• South African Christiaan Barnard performs the first heart transplant in 1967 • UK and France launch the first passenger supersonic flight – *Concorde* – in 1968
Music, film, and theatre	• The Tamla Motown record company arrives on the scene, making mainly black rhythm and blues music with artists such as Aretha Franklin, The Supremes, and Gladys Knight and the Pips
People	• UK children's author Enid Blyton dies in 1968 • Former leader of the Soviet Union, Nikita Khrushchev, dies in 1971 • Marilyn Monroe (below), a movie star popular in the 1950s, dies of an overdose in 1962

GLOSSARY

apartheid system of racial discrimination enforced in South Africa by white only governments until 1994

Arab countries countries in the Middle East, apart from Israel

arms race competition between countries to have more powerful weapons

assassinated deliberately target and kill someone

baby boom period after the Second World War from 1945 to around 1955, when the birth rate increased from previous years

Black Panthers movement in the United States promoting the culture of black people

ceasefire when opposing sides in a war agree to stop fighting for an agreed length of time

chip short for microchip, which is used to make an electronic circuit

civil rights basic entitlements that should belong to citizens. For example, the right to go on strike or to be treated fairly under the law.

civil war war between groups within a country, not a war against another country

Cold War period of hostility between the United States and the USSR that existed from 1945 until the late 1980s

colonist someone who settles in another country in a position of power and owning land

communist someone who believes in government ownership and spreading wealth

compulsory without a choice, something that has to be done

conspiracy theory unproven idea about who is responsible for something

corrupt not honest

councillor elected representative of a community

democracy government where people of the country choose their leaders by voting for them

Democrat member of the Democratic political party in the United States

dictatorship non-democratic system of government where one person or group controls the government

discriminate favour one person or group at the expense of another person or group

disenchanted having lost hope

domino effect idea that a political event or revolution in one country will set off a train of similar events in neighbouring countries

economy matters relating to money

empire control of other countries by a dominant power

ethnic to do with one race or cultural group

flamboyant very showy and eye-catching

flower power flowers became a symbol of peace and love for hippies and the term "flower power" refers to the message and the influence of hippies

guerrilla form of fighting against larger and more powerful forces which avoids an open battle

hippies young people in the 1960s with strong ideas about personal freedom and peace

immigration movement of people into a country from another country

immoral not good, unworthy

impeachment constitutional right of US Congress to put a president on trial, and remove him from office if he is found guilty of an offence against the presidency or the Constitution

Israel country in the Middle East formed in 1948 from land that was previously part of Palestine

Ku Klux Klan (KKK) US white supremacist secret societ that used extreme violence against black people, Jews, Catholics, and immigrants

mass produced made in large quantities

microprocessor circuit, capable of electronic tasks, reduced to a tiny size

Middle East mostly Arab countries located between Europe and Asia

nationalists person with a strong belief in the independence of their country

nationalized not run as a private business for profit, run instead by the government

nuclear weapons most powerful weapons of mass destruction

optimism looking to the future with a sense of hope

PLO Palestine Liberation Organization, developed out of the Israeli occupation of Palestinian territory and fought to establish an independent Palestine

parliament place where politicians make decisions and laws

popular culture way ordinary people enjoy leisure time

post-mortem medical examination into the causes of someone's death

Protestants religious group within Christianity

psychedelic vibrant and multi-coloured

racial segregation treating people differently, and keeping them apart, according to their race

rationing distributing limited supplies on the basis of so much per person

reforms changes designed to improve a situation

refugee person who has no home

Republican member of the Republican political party in the United States

Ska brisk form of Jamaican-born rock derived from reggae and rock, and popularized in the early 1980s by British multi-racial bands

socialist someone who believes in a society that shares profit

Soviet having to do with the USSR

Stock Exchange institution where money is exchanged for shares

superpower very powerful country with a lot of influence, like the United States and the USSR during the Cold War

synthetic made up from different parts, not naturally occurring

trade union organizations formed by workers to protect their interests

Unionist member of the Unionist political party in Northern Ireland

USSR Union of Soviet Socialist Republics

vinyl artificially-made plastic covering

Voting Rights Act law in the United States, passed in 1965, which protected African Americans' right to vote in some southern US states

INDEX

Titles in the *Modern Eras Uncovered* series include:

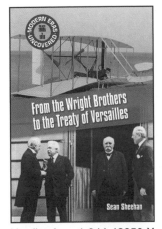

Hardback   1 844 43950 X

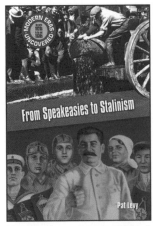

Hardback   1 844 43951 8

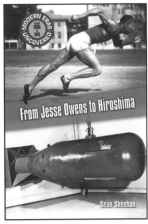

Hardback   1 844 43952 6

Hardback   1 844 43953 4

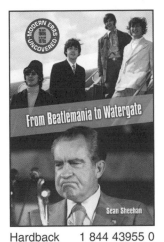

Hardback   1 844 43955 0

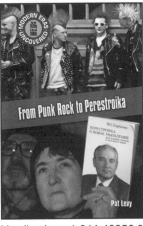

Hardback   1 844 43956 9

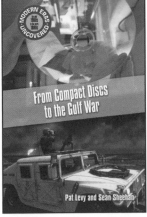

Hardback   1 844 43957 7

Hardback   1 844 43958 5

Find out about the other titles in this series on our website www.raintreepublishers.co.uk